Icebound by Owen Davis

Owen Gould Davis was born on the 29th January 1874 into a large family in Portland, Maine before the family relocated to Bangor where Davis would stay until he was a teenager.

From his early years Davis was an avid playwright and would often write plays for his 8 siblings who would then perform them.

He enrolled at the University of Tennessee in 1888 before transferring to Harvard in 1890 to complete his degree. Whilst there he was an active member of their Society of Arts drama organization.

During his long career Davis wrote some 200 plays, an incredible output by any standard. The first two decades were mainly formulaic melodramas that followed a formula.

'Through the Breakers' his first play, debuted in Bridgeport, Connecticut in 1897 and would run for three years. Davis's first Broadway production opened on 17th September 1900: 'Reaping the Whirlwind' Altogether some 75 Broadway shows were written by him or under his pen-name John Oliver. He would later add the pseudonyms Martin Hurley, Arthur J. Lamb, Walter Lawrence and Robert Wayne.

Soon after he married the actress Elizabeth Drury Breyer, and together they had two sons.

Prior to the First World War, he wrote racy sketches of the high jinks and low life of New York for the Police Gazette under the name of Ike Swift, many were set in the Tenderloin district of Manhattan.

In 1919, he was the first elected president of the Dramatists Guild of America.

A Pulitzer Prize was his achievement in 1923 for his magnificent play 'Icebound'.

Hollywood made the call and Davis went to work at Paramount Pictures for three well paid years working on such films as 'They Had to See Paris' (1929) and 'So This Is London' (1930)'.

Davis also managed to write two autobiographies: 'I'd Like to Do It Again' and 'My First Fifty Years in the Theatre'.

He spent three years of his later life in hospital battling a long-term illness.

On the 13th October 1956, Owen Gould Davis died in New York City at age 82.

Index of Contents

ACT III

FOREWORD

With the production of "The Detour," about a year ago, I managed to secure some measure of success in drawing a simple picture of life as it is lived on a Long Island farm; encouraged by this, I am now turning toward my own people, the people of northern New England, whose folklore, up to the present time, has been quite neglected in our theatre. I mean, of course, that few serious attempts have been made in the direction of a genre comedy of this locality. Here I have at least tried to draw a true picture of these people, and I am of their blood, born of generations of Northern Maine, small-town folk, and brought up among them. In my memory of them is little of the "Rube" caricature of the conventional theatre; they are neither buffoons nor sentimentalists, and at least neither their faults nor their virtues are borrowed from the melting pot but are the direct result of their own heritage and environment.

Owen Davis.
1923.

CAST

"Icebound" was originally produced in New York, February 10, 1923, with the following cast:

Henry Jordan	John Westley
Emma, his wife	Lotta Linthicum
Nettie, her daughter by a former marriage	Boots Wooster
Sadie Fellows, once Sadie Jordan, a widow	Eva Condon
Orin, her son	Andrew J. Lawlor, Jr.
Ella Jordan, the unmarried sister	Frances Neilson
Doctor Curtis	Lawrence Eddinger
Jane Crosby, a second cousin of the Jordans	Phyllis Povah
Judge Bradford	Willard Robertson
Ben Jordan	Robert Ames
Hannah Edna	May Oliver
Jim Jay	Charles Henderson

ACTS & SCENES

ACT ONE
The Parlor of the Jordan Homestead, 4 P.M., October, 1922.
ACT TWO
The Sitting Room of the Jordan Homestead, Two months later. Afternoon.
ACT THREE
Same as Act I, Late in the following March.

ACT ONE

SCENE: The Parlor of the Jordan Homestead at Venzie, Maine

It is late October, and through the two windows at the back one may see a bleak countryside, the grass brown and lifeless, and the bare limbs of the trees silhouetted against a gray sky. Here, in the room that for a hundred years has been the rallying point of the Jordan family, a **GROUP OF RELATIVES** are gathered to await the death of the old woman who is the head of their clan. The room in which they wait is as dull and as drab as the lives of those who have lived within its walls. Here we have the cleanliness that is next to godliness, but no sign of either comfort or beauty, both of which are looked upon with suspicion as being signposts on the road to perdition.

In this group are the following characters: **HENRY JORDAN**, a heavy set man of fifty, worn by his business cares into a dull sort of hopeless resignation. **EMMA**, his wife, a stout and rather formidable woman of forty, with a look of chronic displeasure; **NETTIE**, her daughter by a former marriage, a vain and shallow little rustic beauty; SADIE, a thin, tight-lipped woman of forty, a widow and a gossip; **ORIN**, her son, a pasty-faced boy of ten with large spectacles; **ELLA**, a "Maiden lady" of thirty-six, restless and dissatisfied.

ELLA and **SADIE**, true Jordans by birth, are a degree above **EMMA** in social standing, at least they were until Henry's marriage to **EMMA** made her a somewhat resentful member of the family. In Emma's dialogue and in her reactions, I have attempted a rather nice distinction between the two grades of rural middle-class folk; the younger characters here, as in most other communities, have advanced one step.

Rise: At rise there is a long silence; the occupants of the room are ill at ease. **EMMA** is grim and frowning. Nettie sits with a simper of youthful vanity, looking stealthily at herself from time to time in a small mirror set in the top of her cheap vanity case. **ELLA** and **SADIE** have been crying and dab at their eyes a bit ostentatiously. **HENRY** makes a thoughtful note with a pencil, then returns his notebook to his pocket and warms his hands at the stove.

There is a low whistle of a cold autumn wind as some dead leaves are blown past the window. **ORIN**, who has a cold in his head, sniffs viciously; the others, with the exception of his **MOTHER**, look at him in remonstrance. An eight-day clock in sight, through the door to the hall, strikes four.

EMMA [Sternly]
Four o'clock.

HENRY [Looks at watch]
Five minutes of. That clock's been fast for more 'n thirty years.

NETTIE [Looks at wrist watch]
My watch says two minutes after.

HENRY
Well, it's wrong!

EMMA [Acidly]
You gave it to her yourself, didn't you?

SADIE [Sighs]
Good Land! What does it matter?

NETTIE [Offended]
Oh! Doesn't it? Oh!

ELLA
Maybe it does to you. She ain't your blood relation.

EMMA
Nettie loves her grandma, don't you dear?

NETTIE
Some folks not so far off may get fooled before long about how much grandma and I was to each other.

EMMA [Sternly]
You hush!

[Again there is a pause, and again it is broken by a loud sniff from **ORIN**, as the **WOMEN** look at him in disgust. **SADIE** speaks up in his defense.

SADIE
He's got kind of a cold in his head.

HENRY
The question is, ain't he got a handkerchief?

SADIE
Here, Orin!

[She hands him her handkerchief.

ELLA
The idea! No handkerchief when you've come expectin' someone to die!

ORIN
I had one, but I used it up.

[He blows his nose.

HENRY
After four. Well, I expect they'll have to close the store without me.

ELLA
I left everything just as soon as Jane sent me word!

SADIE
Why should Jane be with her instead of you or me, her own daughters?

HENRY
You girls always made her nervous, and I guess she's pretty low.
[He looks at his watch again]
I said I'd be back before closin' time. I don't know as I dare to trust those boys.

EMMA
You can't tell about things, when Sadie's husband died we sat there most all night.

SADIE [Angrily]
Yes, and you grudged it to him, I knew it then and it isn't likely I'm going to forget it.

ELLA
Will was a good man, but even you can't say he was ever very dependable.

EMMA
My first husband died sudden—
[She turns to **NETTIE**]
—you can't remember it, dear.

ELLA
You didn't remember it very long, it wa'n't much more 'n a year before you married Henry.

HENRY [Sighs]
Well, he was as dead then as he's ever got to be.
[He turns and glances nervously out window]
I don't know but what I could just run down to the store for a minute, then hurry right back.

SADIE
You're the oldest of her children, a body would think you'd be ashamed.

HENRY
Oh, I'll stay.

[There is a silence. **ORIN** sniffs. **ELLA** glares at him.

ELLA
Of course he could sit somewheres else.

[**SADIE** puts her arm about **ORIN** and looks spitefully at **ELLA**. **DOCTOR CURTIS**, an elderly country physician, comes down the stairs and enters the room, all turn to look at him.

DOCTOR
No change at all. I'm sendin' Jane to the drug store.

ELLA [Rises eagerly]
I'll just run up and sit with mother.

[**SADIE** jumps up and starts for door.

SADIE
It might be better if I went.

ELLA
Why might it?

[They stand glaring at each other before either attempts to pass the **DOCTOR**, whose ample form almost blocks the doorway.

SADIE
I've been a wife and a mother.

DOCTOR
Hannah's with her, you know. I told you I didn't want anybody up there but Jane and Hannah.

ELLA
But we're her own daughters.

DOCTOR
You don't have to tell me, I brought both of you into the world. The right nursing might pull her through, even now; nothing else can, and I've got the two women I want.
[He crosses to **HENRY** at stove]
Why don't you put a little wood on the fire?

HENRY
Why—I thought 'twas warm enough.

ELLA
Because you was standin' in front of it gettin' all the heat.

[**HENRY** fills the stove from wood basket.

[**JANE CROSBY** enters on stairs and crosses into the room. **JANE** is twenty-four, a plainly dressed girl of quiet manner. She has been "driven into herself" as one of our characters would describe it, by her lack of sympathy and affection and as a natural result she is not especially articulate; she speaks, as a rule, in short sentences, and has cultivated an outward coldness that in the course of time has become almost aggressive.

JANE
I'll go now, Doctor; you'd better go back to her. Hannah's frightened.

DOCTOR
Get it as quick as you can, Jane; I don't know as it's any use, but we've got to keep on tryin'.

JANE
Yes.

[She exits; **DOCTOR** warms his hands.

DOCTOR
Jane's been up with her three nights. I don't know when I've seen a more dependable girl.

ELLA
She ought to be.

HENRY
If there's any gratitude in the world.

DOCTOR
Oh, I guess there is; maybe there'd be more if there was more reason for it. It's awful cold up there, but I guess I'll be gettin' back.

[He crosses toward door.

HENRY
Doctor!

[He looks at his watch.

DOCTOR [Stops in doorway]
Well?

HENRY
It's quite a bit past four, I don't suppose—I don't suppose you can tell—

DOCTOR
No, I can't tell.

[He turns and exits up the stairs.

ELLA
There's no fool like an old fool.

SADIE
Did you hear him? "Didn't know when he'd seen a more dependable girl than her!"

EMMA
Makes a lot of difference who's goin' to depend on her. I ain't, for one.

NETTIE
If I set out to tell how she's treated me lots of times, when I've come over here to see grandma, nobody would believe a word of it.

SADIE
Mother took her in out of charity.

ELLA
And kept her out of spite.

HENRY
I don't know as you ought to say that, Ella.

ELLA
It's my place she took, in my own mother's house. I'd been here now, but for her. I ain't goin' to forget that. No! Me, all these years payin' board and slavin' my life out, makin' hats, like a nigger.

NETTIE [Smartly]
Oh! So that's what they're like. I've often wondered!

ELLA [Rises]
You'll keep that common little thing of your wife's from insultin' me, Henry Jordan, or I won't stay here another minute.

EMMA [Angry]
Common!

NETTIE
Mother!

HENRY [Sternly]
Hush up! All of yer!

SADIE
It's Jane we ought to be talkin' about.

EMMA
Just as soon as you're the head of the family, Henry, you've got to tell her she ain't wanted here!

HENRY
Well—I don't know as I'd want to do anything that wasn't right. She's been here quite a spell.

SADIE
Eight years!

ELLA
And just a step-cousin, once removed.

HENRY
I guess mother's made her earn her keep. I don't know as ever there was much love lost between 'em.

EMMA
As soon as your mother's dead, you'll send her packing.

HENRY
We'll see. I don't like countin' on mother's going; that way.

SADIE [Hopefully]
Grandmother lived to eighty-four.

HENRY
All our folks was long lived; nothin' lasts like it used to,—Poor mother!

ELLA
Of course she'll divide equal, between us three?

HENRY [Doubtfully]
Well, I don't know!

SADIE
Orin is her only grandchild; she won't forget that.

HENRY
Nettie, there, is just the same as my own. I adopted her legal, when I married Emma.

EMMA
Of course you did. Your mother's too—just a woman to make distinctions!

NETTIE
Yes, and the funny part of it is grandma may leave me a whole lot, for all any of you know.

ELLA
Nonsense! She'll divide equally between us three; won't she, Henry?

HENRY [Sadly]
She'll do as she pleases, I guess we all know that.

ELLA
She's a religious woman, she's got to be fair!

HENRY
Well, I guess it would be fair enough if she was to remember the trouble I've had with my business. I don't know what she's worth, she's as tight-mouthed as a bear trap, but I could use more 'n a third of quite a little sum.

ELLA
Well, you won't get it. Not if I go to law.

EMMA
It's disgusting. Talking about money at a time like this.

HENRY
I like to see folks reasonable. I don't know what you'd want of a third of all mother's got, Ella.

SADIE [To **ELLA**]
You, all alone in the world!

ELLA
Maybe I won't be, when I get that money.

SADIE
You don't mean you'd get married?

EMMA
At your age!

ELLA
I mean I never had anything in all my life; now I'm going to. I'm the youngest of all of you, except Ben, and he never was a real Jordan. I've never had a chance; I've been stuck here till I'm most forty, worse than if I was dead, fifty times worse! Now I'm going to buy things—everything I want—I don't care what—I'll buy it, even if it's a man! Anything I want!

NETTIE
A man!

[**NETTIE** looks at **ELLA** in cruel amazement and all but **ORIN** burst into a laugh—**ELLA** turns up and hides her face against the window as **ORIN** pulls at his mother's skirt.

ORIN
Mum! Mum! I thought you told me not to laugh, not once, while we was here!

HENRY
You're right, nephew, and we're wrong, all of us. I'm sorry, Ella, we're all sorry.

ELLA [Wipes her eyes]
Laugh if you want to—maybe it won't be so long before I do some of it myself.

HENRY [Thoughtfully]
Equally between us three? Well, poor mother knows best of course.

[He sighs.

SADIE

She wouldn't leave him any, would she,—Ben?

ELLA [Shocked]
Ben!

HENRY [In cold anger]
She's a woman of her word; no!

SADIE
If he was here he'd get around her; he always did!

HENRY
Not again!

SADIE
If she ever spoiled anybody it was him, and she's had to pay for it. Sometimes it looks like it was a sort of a judgment.

HENRY
There hasn't been a Jordan, before Ben, who's disgraced the name in more 'n a hundred years; he stands indicted before the Grand Jury for some of his drunken devilment. If he hadn't run away, like the criminal he is, he'd be in the State's Prison now, down to Thomaston. Don't talk Ben to me, after the way he broke mother's heart, and hurt my credit!

NETTIE
I don't remember him very well. Mother thought it better I shouldn't come around last time he was here; but he looked real nice in his uniform.

SADIE
It was his bein' born so long after us that made him seem like an outsider; father and mother hadn't had any children for years and years! Of course I never want to sit in judgment on my own parents, but I never approved of it; it never seemed quite—what I call proper.

NETTIE [To **EMMA**]
Mother, don't you think I'd better leave the room?

SADIE [Angrily]
Not if half the stories I've heard about you are true, I don't.

HENRY
Come, come, no rows! Is this a time or place for spite? We've always been a united family, we've always got to be,—leavin' Ben out, of course. You can't make a silk purse out of a sow's ear.

ORIN
Mum! Say Mum!
[He pulls at **SADIE'S** dress]
Why should anybody want to make a silk purse out of a sow's ear?

ELLA
Can't you stop that boy askin' such fool questions?

SADIE
Well, as far as that goes, why should they? It never sounded reasonable to me.

HENRY [Sternly]
Decent folks don't reason about religion; they just accept it.

ORIN
You could make a skin purse out of a sow's ear, but I'll be darned if you could make a silk purse out of one. I'll bet God couldn't.

HENRY
Are you going to let him talk about God like that, like he was a real person?

ELLA
I don't know as a body could expect any better; his father was a Baptist!

SADIE [Angrily]
His father was a good man, and if he talked about God different from what you do, it was because he knew more about him. And as for my being here at all—
[She rises with her arms about **ORIN**]
—I wouldn't do it, not for anything less than my own mother's deathbed.

HENRY
This family don't ever agree on nothin' but just to differ.

EMMA
As far as I see, the only time you ever get together is when one of you is dead.

ELLA
Maybe that's the reason I got such a feelin' against funerals.

[The outside door opens and Jane enters, a druggist's bottle in her hand; she is followed by **JOHN BRADFORD**, a man of about thirty-five. He is better dressed than any of the others and is a man of a more cosmopolitan type,—a New Englander, but a university man, the local judge and the leading lawyer of the town.

JANE
I met Judge Bradford on the way.

JUDGE JOHN BRADFORD
Court set late. I couldn't get here before. Jane tells me that she's very low.

HENRY
Yes.

JUDGE
I can't realize it; she has always been so strong, so dominant.

ELLA
In the midst of life we are in death.

ORIN
Say, Mum, that's in the Bible too!

SADIE
Hush!

ORIN
Well, ain't it?

SADIE
Will you hush?

HENRY
It's our duty to hope so long as we can.

JUDGE
Yes, of course.

JANE
I'll take this right up.

[She exits up the stairs.

JUDGE [Removes his coat]
I'll wait.

SADIE
She can't see you; she ain't really what a body could call in her right mind.

JUDGE
So Jane said.

[He crosses to stove and warms his hands.

ELLA [Sighs]
It's a sad time for us, Judge!

JUDGE
She was always such a wonderful woman.

HENRY
An awful time for us. Did you come up Main Street, Judge?

JUDGE
Yes.

HENRY
Did you happen to notice if my store was open?

JUDGE
No.

HENRY
Not that it matters—

SADIE
Nothing matters now.

HENRY
No—Mother wasn't ever the kind to neglect things; if the worst does come she'll find herself prepared. Won't she? Won't she, Judge?

JUDGE
Her affairs are, as usual, in perfect order.

HENRY
In every way?

JUDGE [Looks at him coldly]
Her will is drawn and is on deposit in my office, if that is what you mean.

HENRY
Well—that is what I mean—I'm no hypocrite.

EMMA
He's the oldest of the family. He's got a right to ask, hasn't he?

JUDGE
Yes.

HENRY [Honestly]
If I could make her well by givin' up everything I've got in the world, or ever expect to git, I'd do it!

SADIE
All of us would.

HENRY
If it's in my mind at all, as I stand here, that she's a rich woman, it's because my mind's so worried, the way business has been, that I'm drove most frantic; it's because, well—because I'm human; because I can't help it.

ELLA [Bitterly]
You're a man! What do you think it's been for me!

SADIE [With arm about **ORIN**]
His father didn't leave much, you all know that, and it's been scrimp and save till I'm all worn to skin and bone.

ELLA
Just to the three of us, that would be fair.

HENRY
Judge! My brother's name ain't in her will, is it? Tell me that? Ben's name ain't there!

JUDGE
I'd rather not talk about it, Henry.

ELLA
She'd cut him off, she said, the last time he disgraced us, and she's a woman of her word.

SADIE [Eagerly, to **JUDGE**]
And the very next day she sent for you because I was here when she telephoned; and you came to her that very afternoon because I saw you from my front window cross right up to this door.

JUDGE
Possibly. I frequently drop in to discuss business matters with your mother for a moment on my way home.

SADIE
It was five minutes to four when you went in that day, and six minutes to five when you came out, by the clock on my mantel.

JUDGE
Your brother has been gone for almost two years; Your memory is very clear.

ELLA
So's her window.

NETTIE
I know folks in this town that are scared to go past it.

SADIE [To her]
I know others that ought to be.

HENRY [Discouraged]
Every time you folks meet there's trouble.

[**JANE** enters down the stairs and into the room.

JUDGE [Looks at her]
Well, Jane?

JANE
No change. It's—it's pitiful, to see her like that.

[**SADIE** sobs and covers her face.

HENRY
It's best we should try to bear this without any fuss, she'd 'a' wanted it that way.

SADIE
She didn't even want me to cry when poor Will died, but I did; and somehow I don't know but it made things easier.

HENRY
When father died she didn't shed a tear; she's been a strong woman, always.

[The early fall twilight has come on and the stage is rather dim, the hall at R. is in deep shadow, at the end of Henry's speech the outside door supposedly out at R. is open, then shut rather violently.

ELLA [Startled]
Someone's come in.

SADIE
Nobody's got any right—

[She rises as some one is heard coming along the hall.

HENRY [Sternly]
Who's that out there? Who is it?

ORIN
Mum! Who is it!

[He clings to his **MOTHER** afraid, as all turn to the door, and **BEN JORDAN** steps into the room and faces them with a smile of reckless contempt. **BEN** is the black sheep of the Jordan family, years younger than any of the others, a wild, selfish, arrogant fellow, handsome but sulky and defiant. His clothes are cheap and dirty and he is rather pale and looks dissipated. He doesn't speak but stands openly sneering at their look of astonishment.

JANE [Quietly]
I'm glad you've come, Ben.

BEN [Contemptuously]
You are?

JANE
Yes, your mother's awful sick.

BEN
She's alive?

JANE
Yes.

BEN
Well—
[He looks contemptuously about]
Nobody missin'. The Jordans are gathered again, handkerchiefs and all.

HENRY
You'll be arrested soon as folks know you've come.

BEN [Scornfully]
And I suppose you wouldn't bail me out, would you, Henry?

HENRY [Simply]
No, I wouldn't.

BEN
God! You're still the same, all of you. You stink of the Ark, the whole tribe. It takes more than a few Edisons to change the Jordans!

ELLA
How'd you get here? How'd you know about mother?

BEN [Nods at **JANE**]
She sent me word, to Bangor.

SADIE [To **JANE**]
How'd you get to know where he was?

JANE [Quietly]
I knew.

HENRY
How'd you come; you don't look like you had much money?

BEN
She sent it.
[He nods toward **JANE**]
God knows, it wasn't much.

ELLA [To **JANE**]

Did mother tell you to—?

BEN
Of course she did!

JANE [Quietly]
No, she didn't.

HENRY
You sent your own money?

JANE
Yes, as he said it wasn't much, but I didn't have much.

BEN [Astonished]
Why did you do it?

JANE
I knew she was going to die; twice I asked her if she wanted to see you, and she said no—

HENRY
And yet you sent for him?

JANE
Yes.

HENRY
Why?

JANE
He was the one she really wanted. I thought she'd die happier seeing him.

ELLA
You took a lot on yourself, didn't you?

JANE
Yes, she's been a lonely old woman. I hated to think of her there, in the churchyard, hungry for him.

BEN
I'll go to her.

JANE
It's too late; she wouldn't know you.

BEN
I'll go.

JANE

The doctor will call us when he thinks we ought to come.

BEN [Fiercely]
I'm going now.

HENRY [Steps forward]
No, you ain't.

BEN
Do you think I came here, standin' a chance of bein' sent to jail, to let you tell me what to do?

HENRY
If she's dyin' up there, it's more'n half from what you've made her suffer; you'll wait here till we go to her together.

EMMA
Henry's right.

SADIE
Of course he is.

ELLA
Nobody but Ben would have the impudence to show his face here, after what he's done.

BEN
I'm going just the same!

HENRY
No, you ain't.

[Their voices become loud.

EMMA
Henry! Don't let him go!

SADIE
Stop him.

ELLA [Grows shrill]
He's a disgrace to us. He always was.

HENRY
You'll stay right where you are.

[He puts his hand heavily on Ben's shoulder—**BEN** throws him off fiercely.

BEN
Damn you! Keep your hands off me!

[**HENRY** staggers back and strikes against a table that falls to the floor with a crash. **NETTIE** screams.

JANE
Stop it—stop! You must!

JUDGE
Are you crazy? Have you no sense of decency?

[**DOCTOR CURTIS** comes quickly downstairs.

DOCTOR
What's this noise? I forbid it. Your mother has heard you.

HENRY [Ashamed]
I'm sorry.

BEN [Sulkily]
I didn't mean to make a row.

HENRY
It's him.
[He looks bitterly at **BEN**]
He brings out all the worst in us. He brought trouble into the world with him when he came, and ever since.

[**HANNAH**, a middle-aged servant, comes hastily half-way downstairs and calls out sharply.

HANNAH
Doctor! Come, Doctor!

[She exits up the stairs, as the **DOCTOR** crosses through the hall and follows her.

ORIN [Afraid]
Is she dead, Mum? Does Hannah mean she's dead!

[**SADIE** hides her head on his shoulder and weeps.

JANE
I'll go to her.

[She exits.

ELLA [Violently]
She'll go. There ain't scarcely a drop of Jordan blood in her veins, and she's the one that goes to mother.

EMMA [Coldly]
Light the lamp, Nettie; it's gettin' dark.

NETTIE
Yes, mother.

[She starts to light lamp.

HENRY
I'm ashamed of my part of it, makin' a row, with her on her deathbed.

BEN
You had it right, I guess. I've made trouble ever since I came into the world.

NETTIE
There!

[She lights lamp; footlights go up.

JUDGE [Sternly]
You shouldn't have come here; you know that, Ben.

BEN
I've always known that, any place I've been, exceptin' only those two years in the Army. That's the only time I ever was in right.

JUDGE [Sternly]
I would find it easier to pity you if you had any one to blame besides yourself.

BEN
Pity? Do you think I want your pity?

[There is a pause.

[**JANE** is seen on stairs, they all turn to her nervously as she comes down and crosses into room. She stops at the door looking at them.

HENRY [Slowly]
Mother—mother's—gone!

JANE
Yes.

[There is a moment's silence broken by the low sobs of the **WOMEN** who for a moment forget their selfishness in the presence of death.

HENRY
The Jordans won't ever be the same; she was the last of the old stock, mother was—No, the Jordans won't ever be the same.

[**DOCTOR CURTIS** comes downstairs and into the room.

DOCTOR
It's no use tryin' to tell you what I feel. I've known her since I was a boy. I did the best I could.

HENRY
The best anybody could, Doctor, we know that.

DOCTOR
I've got a call I'd better make—
[He looks at watch]
—should have been there hours ago, but I hadn't the heart to leave her. Who's in charge here?

HENRY
I am, of course.

DOCTOR
I've made arrangements with Hannah; she'll tell you.
I'll say good night now.

HENRY
Good night, Doctor.

JANE
And thank you.

DOCTOR
We did our best, Jane.

[He exits.

SADIE
He's gettin' old. When Orin had the stomach trouble a month ago, I sent for Doctor Morris. I felt sort of guilty doin' it, but I thought it was my duty.

JUDGE
You will let me help you, Jane?

JANE
Hannah and I can attend to everything. Henry!
[She turns to him]
You might come over for a minute this evening and we can talk things over. I'll make the bed up in your old room, Ben, if you want to stay.

EMMA [Rises and looks at Jane coldly]
Now, Henry Jordan, if she's all through givin' orders, maybe you'll begin.

ELLA

Well, I should say so. Let's have an understandin'.

SADIE
You tell her the truth, Henry, or else one of us will do it for you.

HENRY [Hesitates]
Maybe it might be best if I should wait until after the funeral.

ELLA
You tell her now, or I will.

JANE
Tell me what?

HENRY
We was thinkin' now that mother's dead, that there wasn't much use in your stayin' on here.

JANE
Yes?

[She looks at him intently.

HENRY
We don't aim to be hard, and we don't want it said we was mean about it; you can stay on here, if you want to, until after the funeral, maybe a little longer, and I don't know but what between us, we'd be willing to help you till you found a place somewheres.

JANE
You can't help me, any of you. Of course now she's dead, I'll go. I'll be glad to go.

ELLA
Glad!

JANE [Turns on them]
I hate you, the whole raft of you. I'll be glad to get away from you. She was the only one of you worth loving, and she didn't want it.

EMMA
If that's how you feel, I say the sooner you went the better.

HENRY
Not till after the funeral. I don't want it said we was hard to her.

JUDGE [Quietly]
Jane isn't going at all, Henry.

HENRY
What's that?

ELLA
Of course she's going.

JUDGE
No, she belongs here in this house.

HENRY
Not after I say she don't.

JUDGE
Even then, because it's hers.

SADIE
Hers?

JUDGE
From the moment of your mother's death, everything here belonged to Jane.

HENRY
Not everything.

JUDGE
Yes, everything—your mother's whole estate.

BEN
Ha! Ha! Ha!

[He sits at right laughing bitterly.

JANE
That can't be, Judge, you must be wrong. It's a mistake.

JUDGE
No.

HENRY
My mother did this?

JUDGE
Yes.

HENRY
Why? You've got to tell me why!

JUDGE
That isn't a part of my duties.

HENRY
She couldn't have done a thing like that without sayin' why. She said something, didn't she?

JUDGE
I don't know that I care to repeat it.

HENRY [Fiercely]
You must repeat it!

JUDGE
Very well. The day that will was drawn she said to me, "The Jordans are all waiting for me to die, like carrion crows around a sick cow in a pasture, watchin' till the last twitch of life is out of me before they pounce. I'm going to fool them," she said, "I'm going to surprise them; they are all fools but Jane—Jane's no fool."

BEN [Bitterly]
No—Ha! Ha! Ha! Jane's no fool!

JUDGE
And she went on—
[He turns to **JANE**]
You'll forgive me Jane; she said, "Jane is stubborn, and set, and wilful, but she's no fool. She'll do better by the Jordan money than any of them."

ELLA
We'll go to law, that's what we'll do!

SADIE
That's it, we'll go to law.

HENRY [To **JUDGE**]
We can break that will; you know we can!

JUDGE
It's possible.

HENRY
Possible! You know, don't yer! You're supposed to be a good lawyer.

JUDGE
Of course if I am a good lawyer you can't break that will, because you see I drew it.

ELLA
And we get nothing, not a dollar, after waitin' all these years?

JUDGE
There are small bequests left to each of you.

SADIE
How much?

JUDGE
One hundred dollars each.

ELLA [Shrilly]
One hundred dollars.

JUDGE
I said that they were small.

BEN
You said a mouthful!

ELLA
Ha! Ha! Ha! Ha! Ha!

[She laughs wildly.

HENRY [Sternly]
Stop your noise, Ella.

ELLA
I—Ha! Ha! Ha!—I told you I was going to have my laugh, didn't I? Ha! Ha! Ha!

ORIN [Pulls **SADIE'S** dress]
Mum! What's she laughin' for?

SADIE
You hush!

EMMA [Faces them all in evil triumph]
If anybody asked me, I'd say it was a judgment on all of yer. You Jordans was always stuck up, always thought you was better'n anybody else. I guess I ought to know, I married into yer!—You a rich family?—You the salt of the Earth—You Jordans! You paupers—Ha! Ha! Ha!

ORIN [Pulls **SADIE'S** skirt]
Ain't she still dead, Mum! Ain't grandma still dead?

SADIE [Angrily]
Of course she is.

ORIN
But I thought we was all goin' to cry!

SADIE
Cry then, you awful little brat.

[She slaps his face and he roars loudly; she takes him by the arm and yanks him out of the room, followed by **HENRY**, **EMMA**, **NETTIE** and **ELLA**—through his roars, they all speak together as they go.

EMMA [To **HENRY**]
One hundred dollars! After all your blowin'.

HENRY
It's you, and that child of your'n; you turned her against me.

NETTIE
Well, I just won't spend my hundred dollars for mournin'. I'll wear my old black dress!

ELLA
And me makin' hats all the rest of my life—just makin' hats!

[The front door is heard to shut behind them. **JANE**, **BEN** and **JUDGE** are alone. **JUDGE** stands by stove. **JANE** is up by window, looking out at the deepening twilight. **BEN** sits at right.

BEN
Ha! Ha! Ha! "Crow buzzards" mother called us—the last of the Jordans—crow buzzards—and that's what we are.

JUDGE
You can't stay here, Ben; you know that as well as I do. I signed the warrant for your arrest myself. It's been over a year since the Grand Jury indicted you for arson.

BEN
You mean you'll give me up?

JANE
You won't do that, Judge; you're here as her friend.

JUDGE
No, but if it's known he's here, I couldn't save him, and it's bound to be known.

JANE [To **BEN**]
Were you careful coming?

BEN
Yes.

JUDGE
It's bound to be known.

BEN
He means they'll tell on me.
[He nods his head toward door]

My brother, or my sisters.

JUDGE
No, I don't think they'd do that.

BEN
Let 'em! What do I care. I'm sick of hiding out, half starved! Let 'em do what they please. All I know is one thing,—when they put her into her grave her sons and daughters are goin' to be standin' there, like the Jordans always do.

JANE [Quietly]
Hannah will have your room ready by now. There are some clean shirts and things that was your father's; I'll bring them to you.

BEN [Uneasily]
Can I go up there, just a minute?

JANE
To your mother?

BEN
Yes.

JANE
If you want to.

BEN
I do.

JANE
Yes, you can go.

[**BEN** turns and exits up the stairs. **JANE** crosses and sits by stove, sinking wearily into the chair.

JUDGE
And she left him nothing, just that hundred dollars, and only that because I told her it was the safest way to do it. I thought he was her one weakness, but it seems she didn't have any.

JANE
No.

JUDGE
She was a grim old woman, Jane.

JANE
I think I could have loved her, but she didn't want it.

JUDGE

And yet she left you everything.

JANE
I don't understand.

JUDGE
She left a sealed letter for you. It's in my strong box; you may learn from it that she cared more about you than you think.

JANE
No.

JUDGE
There was more kindness in her heart than most people gave her credit for.

JANE
For her own, for Uncle Ned, who never did for her, for Ned, for the Jordan name. I don't understand, and I don't think I care so very much; it's been a hard week, Judge.

[She rests her head against the back of the chair.

JUDGE
I know, and you're all worn out.

JANE
Yes.

JUDGE
It's a lot of money, Jane.

JANE
I suppose so.

JUDGE
And so you're a rich woman. I am curious to know how you feel?

JANE
Just tired.

[She shuts her eyes. For a moment he looks at her with a smile, then turns and quietly fills the stove with wood as **BEN** comes slowly downstairs and into the room.

BEN
If there was only something I could do for her.

JUDGE
Jane's asleep, Ben.

BEN
Did she look like that, unhappy, all the time?

JUDGE
Yes.

BEN
Crow buzzards! God damn the Jordans!

[Front door bell rings sharply, **BEN** is startled.

JUDGE
Steady there! It's just one of the neighbors, I guess.

[Bell rings again as **HANNAH** crosses downstairs and to hall.

Hannah knows enough not to let any one in.

BEN [Slowly]
When I got back, time before this, from France, I tried to go straight, but it wasn't any good, I just don't belong—

[**HANNAH** enters frightened.

HANNAH
It's Jim Jay!

BEN [To **JUDGE**]
And you didn't think my own blood would sell me?

[**JIM JAY**, a large, kindly man of middle age, enters.

JIM
I'm sorry, Ben, I've come for you!

[**JANE** wakes, startled, and springs up.

JANE
What is it?

JIM
I got to take him, Jane.

BEN [Turns fiercely]
Have you!

JIM [Quietly]
I'm armed, Ben—better not be foolish!

JANE
He'll go with you, Mr. Jay. He won't resist.

JIM [Quietly]
He mustn't. You got a bad name, Ben, and I ain't a-goin' to take any chances.

BEN
I thought I'd get to go to her funeral, anyway, before they got me.

JIM
Well, you could, maybe, if you was to fix a bail bond. You'd take bail for him, wouldn't you, Judge?

JUDGE
It's a felony; I'd have to have good security.

JANE
I'm a rich woman, you said just now. Could I give bail for him?

JUDGE
Yes.

BEN [To her]
So the money ain't enough. You want all us Jordans fawnin' on you for favors. Well, all of 'em but me will; by mornin' the buzzards will be flocking round you thick! You're going to hear a lot about how much folks love you, but you ain't goin' to hear it from me.

JANE [Turns to him quietly]
Why did you come here, Ben, when I wrote you she was dying?

BEN
Why did I come?

JANE
Was it because you loved her, because you wanted to ask her to forgive you, before she died—or was it because you wanted to get something for yourself?

BEN [Hesitates]
How does a feller know why he does what he does?

JANE
I'm just curious. You've got so much contempt for the rest, I was just wondering? You were wild, Ben, and hard, but you were honest—what brought you here?

BEN [Sulkily]
The money.

JANE

I thought so. Then when you saw her you were sorry, but even then the money was in your mind—well—it's mine now. And you've got to take your choice,—you can do what I tell you, or you'll go with Mr. Jay.

BEN
Is that so? Well I guess there ain't much doubt about what I'll do. Come on, Jim?

JIM
All right.
[He takes a pair of handcuffs from his pocket]
You'll have to slip these on, Ben.

BEN [Steps back]
No—wait—
[He turns desperately to **JANE**]
What is it you want?

JANE
I want you to do as I say.

BEN [After a look at **JIM** and the handcuffs]
I'll do it.

JANE
I thought so.
[She turns to **JUDGE**]
Can you fix the bond up here?

JUDGE
Yes.
[He sits at table and takes pen, ink and paper from a drawer]
I can hold court right here long enough for that.

JIM
This is my prisoner, Judge, and here's the warrant.

[He puts warrant on table.

JANE
First he's got to swear, before you, to my conditions.

BEN
What conditions?

JANE
When will his trial be, Judge?

JUDGE

Not before the spring term, I should think—say early April.

JANE
You'll stay here till then, Ben; you won't leave town! You'll work the farm,—there's plenty to be done.

BEN [Sulkily]
I don't know how to work a farm.

JANE
I do. You'll just do what I tell you.

BEN
Be your slave? That's what you mean, ain't it?

JANE
I've been about that here for eight years.

BEN
And now it's your turn to get square on a Jordan!

JANE
You'll work for once, and work every day. The first day you don't I'll surrender you to the judge, and he'll jail you. The rest of the Jordans will live as I tell them to live, or for the first time in any of their lives, they'll live on what they earn. Don't forget, Ben, that right now I'm the head of the family.

JUDGE [To **BEN**]
You heard the conditions? Shall I make out the bond?

BEN [Reluctantly]
Yes.

[He sits moodily at right, looking down at the floor. **JANE** looks at him for a moment, then turns up to window.

JANE
It's snowing!

JIM
Thought I smelled it.
[He buttons his coat]
Well, nothin' to keep me, is there, Judge?

JUDGE
No.
[He starts to write out the bond with a rusty pen]
This pen is rusty!

JIM

I was sorry to hear about the old lady. It's too bad, but that's the way of things.

JUDGE [Writes]
Yes.

JIM
Well—It's early for snow, not but what it's a good thing for the winter wheat.

[He exits.

ACT TWO

SCENE: Sitting room of the Jordan homestead some two months later.

This room also shows some traces of a family's daily life, and to that extent is less desolate than the "parlor" of the first act, although the stern faith of the Puritan makes no concession to the thing we have learned to call "good taste." The old-fashioned simplicity seen in such a room as this has resulted from poverty, both of mind and of purse, and has nothing akin to the simplicity of the artist; as a matter of fact, your true descendant of the settlers of 1605 would be the first to resent such an implication; to them the arts are directly connected with heathen practices, and any incense burned before the altars of the Graces still smells to them of brimstone.

At back center folding doors, now partly open, lead to dining room. In this room may be seen the dining table, back of the table a window looking out on to the farm yard, now deep in midwinter snow. At right is an open fireplace with a log fire. Below fireplace a door to hall. Up left door to small vestibule in which is the outside door. Down left a window overlooking a snowbound countryside. The clock above the fireplace is set for quarter past four. Several straight-backed chairs and a woodbox by fireplaces. A sewing table and lamp at center. A sewing machine near window at left. A wall cupboard on the wall right of the doors to the dining room. An old sofa down left, two chairs at right. When the door at left, in vestibule, is opened, one may see a path up to the door, between two walls of snow.

Discovered: **ELLA** sits right at sewing machine, hemming some rough towels. **ORIN** and **NETTIE** are by fireplace. **SADIE** sits right of center. **SADIE** and **ORIN** are dressed for outdoors. Nettie's coat, hat and overshoes are on a hat-rack by door at left. **ORIN**, as the curtain goes up, is putting a log on the fire.

SADIE [Acidly to **ELLA**]
Why shouldn't he put wood on the fire if he wants to?

ELLA [At sewing machine]
Because it ain't your wood.

SADIE
No, it's hers! Everything is hers!

ELLA

And maybe she just don't know it.

NETTIE [At fireplace]
Ah!
[She bends closer to the fire as the log blazes up]
I do love a good fire! Oh it's nice to be warm!

SADIE
There's somethin' sensual about it.

NETTIE
Mother told me that the next time you started talkin' indecent I was to leave the room.

SADIE
Tell your mother I don't wonder she's sort of worried about you. I'd be if you was my daughter.

ELLA
I don't see why you can't let Nettie alone!

NETTIE
She's always picking on me, Aunt Ella! To hear her talk anybody would think I was terrible.

SADIE
I know more about what's going on than some folks think I do.

NETTIE
Then you know a lot. I heard Horace Bevins say a week ago that he didn't know as it was any use tryin' to have a Masonic Lodge in the same town as you.

SADIE
They never was a Bevins yet didn't have his tongue hung from the middle; the day his mother was married she answered both the responses.

ORIN
Mum! Mum! Shall I take my coat off; are we going to stay, Mum?

SADIE
No, we ain't going to stay. I just want to see Cousin Jane for a minute.

ELLA
She's in the kitchen with Hannah.

SADIE
Watchin' her, I bet! I wonder Hannah puts up with it.

ELLA
If you was to live with Jane for a spell, I guess you'd find you had a plenty to put up with.

SADIE
It's enough to make the Jordans turn in their graves, all of 'em at once.

ELLA
I guess all she'd say would be, "Let 'em if it seemed to make 'em any more comfortable."

[**JANE** enters. She has apron on and some towels over her arm.

JANE
Are those towels finished?

ELLA
Some is! Maybe I'd done all of 'em if I'd been a centipede.

JANE
Oh! I didn't see you, Sadie.

SADIE
Oh! Ha, ha! Well, I ain't surprised.

JANE [With **ELLA**, selecting finished towels]
Well, Orin, does the tooth still hurt you?

ORIN
Naw, it don't hurt me none now. I got it in a bottle.

[He takes small bottle from pocket.

NETTIE
Oh you nasty thing. You get away!

SADIE [Angrily]
What did I tell you about showin' that tooth to folks!

JANE
Never mind, Orin, just run out to the barn and tell your Uncle Ben we've got to have a path cleared under the clothes-lines.

ORIN
All right.

[He crosses toward door.

JANE
Hannah's going to wash to-morrow, tell him. I'll expect a good wide path.

ORIN
I'll tell him.

[He exits.

SADIE
I must say you keep Ben right at it, don't you?

JANE
Yes.
[She takes the last finished towel and speaks to **ELLA**]
I'll come back for more.

SADIE [As **JANE** crosses]
First I thought he'd go to jail before he'd work, but he didn't, did he?

JANE
No.

[She exits right.

SADIE
Yes. No! Yes. No! Folks that ain't got no more gift of gab ain't got much gift of intellect. I s'pose Hannah's out there.

ELLA
Yes, she keeps all of us just everlastingly at it.

SADIE
When Jane comes back, I wish you and Nettie would leave me alone with her, just for a minute.

ELLA [As she works over sewing machine]
It won't do you much good; she won't lend any more money.

SADIE
Mother always helped me. I've got a right to expect it.

ELLA [As she bites off a thread]
Expectin' ain't gettin'.

SADIE
I don't know what I'll do.

ELLA
You had money out of her; so has Henry.

SADIE [Shocked, to **NETTIE**]
You don't mean to say your father's been borrowin' from her.

NETTIE

He's always borrowin'. Didn't he borrow the hundred dollars grandma left me? I'm not going to stand it much longer.

ELLA
Henry's havin' trouble with his business.

SADIE
We're fools to put up with it. Everybody says so. We ought to contest the will.

ELLA
Everybody says so but the lawyers; they won't none of 'em touch the case without they get money in advance.

SADIE
How much money? Didn't your father find out, Nettie?

NETTIE
The least was five hundred dollars.

ELLA
Can you see us raisin' that?

SADIE
If we was short, we might borrow it from Jane.

ELLA
We'd have to be smarter'n I see any signs of; she's through lendin'.

SADIE
How do you know?

ELLA
I tried it myself.

SADIE
What do you want money for. Ain't she takin' you in to live with her?

ELLA
I don't call myself beholden for that. She had to have some one, with Ben here, and her unmarried, and next to no relation to him.

NETTIE
Everybody's callin' you the chaperon!
[She laughs]
Not but what they ought to be one with him around; he's awful good lookin'.

SADIE

You keep away from him. He's no blood kin of yours, and he's a bad man, if he is a Jordan. Always makes up to everything he sees in petticoats, and always did.

NETTIE
Thanks for the compliment, but I'm not looking for any jailbirds.

ELLA
It will be awful, Ben in State's Prison,—and I guess he'll have to go, soon as he stands his trial.

SADIE
He got drunk and had a fight with the two Kimbal boys, and they licked him, and that night he burned down their barn; everybody knows it.

ELLA
He's bad, all through, Ben is.

NETTIE
He'll get about five years, father says. I guess that will take some of the spunk out of him.

[A sound in the hall at right.

ELLA
Hush! I think he's coming.

[**BEN** enters at right with a big armful of firewood and crosses and drops it heavily into woodbox, then turns and looks at them in silence.

SADIE
Seems kind of funny, your luggin' in the wood.

BEN [Bitterly]
Does it?

SADIE
Did you see Orin out there?

BEN
Yes, he went along home.

SADIE
How do you like workin'?

BEN
How do you think I like it? Workin' a big farm in winter, tendin' the stock and milking ten cows. How do I like it?

[As he stands by fire **NETTIE** looks up at him.

NETTIE
I think it's just a shame!

SADIE [Turns to **ELLA**]
Are you going to make towels all the afternoon?

ELLA
I am 'til they're done, then I expect she'll find somethin' else for me to do.

NETTIE [To **BEN**]
Do you know I'm sorry for you, awful sorry.

[She speaks low. **ELLA** and **SADIE** are at the other side of room.

BEN
Then you're the only one.

NETTIE
Maybe I am, but I'm like that.

BEN
Another month of it, then State's Prison, I guess. I don't know as I'll be sorry when the time comes.

NETTIE
Oh, Uncle Ben! No, I'm not goin' to call you that. After all, you're not really any relation, are you? I mean to me?

BEN
No.

NETTIE [Softly]
I'm just going to call you Ben!

BEN
You're a good kid, Nettie.

NETTIE
Oh, it isn't that, Ben, but it does just seem too awful.

[As she looks up at him, the outside door opens and **HENRY** and **EMMA** enter. They see **NETTIE** and **BEN** together by the fire.

EMMA [Sternly]
Nettie!

NETTIE [Sweetly]
Yes, mother?

EMMA
You come away from him.

BEN [Angrily]
What do you mean by that?

EMMA
You tell him, Henry.

HENRY
I don't know as it's any use to—

EMMA [Sternly]
Tell him what I mean.

HENRY [To **BEN**]
Emma thinks, considerin' everything, that it's best Nettie shouldn't talk to you.

BEN
Why don't you keep her at home then? You don't suppose I want to talk to her.

EMMA
Oh, we ain't wanted here, I guess. We know that, not by you, or by her;—and Henry's the oldest of the Jordans. All this would be his, if there was any justice in the world.

NETTIE
Father wouldn't have taken that hundred dollars grandma left me if there had been any justice in the world. That's what I came here for, not to talk to him. To tell Cousin Jane what father did, and to tell her about Nellie Namlin's Christmas party, and that I've got to have a new dress. I've just got to!

SADIE
A new dress, and my rent ain't paid. She's got to pay it. My Orin's got to have a roof over his head.

HENRY
I don't know as you've got any call to be pestering Jane all the time.

ELLA
She's always wantin' something.

SADIE
What about you? Didn't you tell me yourself you tried to borrow from her?

ELLA
I got a chance to set up in business, so as I can be independent. I can go in with Mary Stanton, dressmakin'. I can do it for two hundred dollars, and she's got to give it to me.

HENRY

You ought to be ashamed, all three of you, worryin' Jane all day long. It's more'n flesh and blood can stand!

NETTIE [To him]
Didn't you say at breakfast you was coming here to-day to make Cousin Jane endorse a note for you? Didn't you?

EMMA [Fiercely]
You hush!

BEN [At back by window]
Ha! Ha! Ha! Crow buzzards.

HENRY
Endorsing a note ain't lending money, is it? It's a matter of business. I guess my note's good.

BEN
Take it to the bank without her name on it and see how good it is.

EMMA
You don't think we want to ask her favors, but Henry's in bad trouble and she'll just have to help us this time.

BEN
There's one way out of your troubles. One thing you could all do, for a change, instead of making Jane pay all your bills. I wonder you haven't any of you thought of it.

HENRY
What could we do?

BEN
Go to work and earn something for yourselves.

SADIE
Like you do, I suppose.

EMMA
The laughing-stock of all Veazie!

ELLA
Everybody's talkin' about it, anywhere you go.

NETTIE
Jane Crosby's White Slave, that's what they call you. Jane Crosby's White Slave.

BEN [Fiercely]
They call me that, do they?

ELLA [To **NETTIE**]
Why can't you ever hold your tongue?

BEN [In cold anger]
I've been a damned fool. I'm through.

[**HANNAH** enters.

HANNAH
She wants you.

BEN
Jane?

HANNAH
Yes.

BEN
I won't come.

HANNAH
There'll be another row.

BEN
Tell her I said I wouldn't come.

[He sits.

HANNAH
She's awful set, you know, when she wants anything.

BEN
You tell her I won't come.

HANNAH
Well, I don't say I hanker none to tell her, but I'd rather be in my shoes than your'n.

[She exits.

SADIE
Well, I must say I don't blame you a mite.

EMMA
If the Jordans is a lot of slaves, I guess it's pretty near time we knew it.

HENRY [Worried]
She'll turn you over to Judge Bradford, Ben; he'll lock you up. It ain't goin' to help me none with the bank, a brother of mine bein' in jail.

BEN

So they're laughing at me, are they, damn them.

NETTIE [At door right]

She's coming!

[There is a moment's pause and Jane enters door right. **HANNAH** follows to door and looks on eagerly.

JANE

I sent for you, Ben.

BEN

I won't budge.

JANE [Wearily]

Must we go through all this again?

BEN

I ain't going to move out of this chair to-day. You do what you damned please.

JANE

I am sorry, but you must.

BEN

Send for Jim Jay, have me locked up, do as you please. Oh, I've said it before, but this time I mean it.

JANE

And you won't come?

BEN

No.

JANE

Then I'll do the best I can alone.

[She crosses up to wall closet and opens it and selects a large bottle, and turns. **BEN** rises quickly.

BEN

What do you want of that?

JANE

It's one of the horses. I don't know what's the matter with her. She's down in her stall, just breathing. She won't pay any attention to me.

BEN

Old Nellie?

JANE
Yes.

BEN
What you got?
[He steps to her and takes the bottle from her and looks at it]
That stuff's no good. Here!
[He steps to cabinet and selects another bottle]
If you hadn't spent five minutes stalling around, I might have had a better chance.

[He exits quickly at left.

HANNAH
I allers said 'twas easier to catch flies with honey than 'twas with vinegar.

HENRY
What's Ben know about horses?

JANE
A lot.

HENRY
I didn't know that.

JANE
Neither did Ben, six weeks ago.

[She exits.

HENRY
Mother was like that, about animals. I guess Ben sort of takes after her.

EMMA [Shocked]
Ben! Like your mother!

HANNAH
Of course he is. He's the "spit and image of her."

[She exits.

NETTIE
She made him go! It wouldn't surprise me a mite if she'd pushed that old horse over herself.

[JANE enters.

JANE

He wouldn't let me in the barn.
[For the first time in the play, she laughs lightly]
Well—
[She looks about at them]
We have quite a family gathering here this afternoon. I am wondering if there is any—special reason for it?

HENRY
I wanted to talk with yer for just a minute, Jane.

SADIE
So do I.

JANE
Anybody else?

[She looks about.

ELLA
I do.

NETTIE
So do I.

JANE
I've a lot to do; suppose I answer you all at once. I'm sorry, but I won't lend you any money.

HENRY
Of course, I didn't think they'd call that note of mine; it's only five hundred, and you could just endorse it.

JANE
No!

SADIE
I was going to ask you—

JANE
No!

ELLA
I got a chance to be independent, Jane, and—No. I haven't any money. I won't have before the first of the month.

EMMA
No money!

HENRY

I bet you're worth as much to-day as you was the day mother died.

JANE
To a penny. I've lived, and run this house, and half supported all of you on what I've made the place earn. Yesterday I spent the first dollar that I didn't have to spend. I mean, on myself. But that's no business of yours. I am worth just as much as the day I took the property, and I'm not going to run behind, so you see, after all, I'm a real Jordan.

EMMA
Seems so. I never knew one of 'em yet who didn't seem to think he could take it with him.

HENRY
Well, Jane, I don't know as it's any use tryin' to get you to change your mind?

JANE
I'm sorry.

EMMA
You can leave that for us to be. I guess it's about the only thing we've got a right to. Get your things on, Nettie!

NETTIE
I'm going to stay a while with Aunt Ella; I won't be late.

HENRY
I don't know what I'm goin' to do about that note. I s'pose I'll find some way out of it.

JANE
I hope so.

EMMA
Thank yer. Of course we know there's always the poorhouse. Come, Henry.

[She exits at left, leaving the outside door open.

HENRY
Emma is a little upset. I hope you won't mind her talk. I guess her part of it ain't any too easy.

[He exits, shutting the door.

ELLA [To **JANE**]
Poor Henry! Of course I s'pose you're right not to lend it to him. But I don't know as I could do it, but I'm sensitive.

JANE
Perhaps it's harder to say no than you think.

[**HANNAH** enters.

HANNAH
I got everything ready for to-morrow's wash, but the sheets off your bed, Miss Ella.

ELLA
Good Land! I forgot 'em. Nettie will bring 'em right down.

NETTIE [To **JANE**]
After that, I'm going to stay and help Aunt Ella. I was wondering if you'd be here all the afternoon.

JANE
Yes.

NETTIE [Charmingly]
Nothing special, you know. I'd just like to have a little visit with you.

[She exits at left with **ELLA**.

HANNAH [Looks after her]
Every time I listen to that girl I get fur on my tongue.

JANE
Fur?

HANNAH
Like when my dyspepsia's coming. There's two things I can't abide, her and cucumbers.

[She crosses to door left.

JANE
Hannah!

HANNAH [Stops]
Well?

JANE [Rather shyly]
We are going to have rather a special supper to-night.

HANNAH [Doubtfully]
We are?

JANE
Yes. That's why I had you roast that turkey yesterday.

HANNAH [Firmly]
That's for Sunday!

JANE

No, it's for to-night.

HANNAH [Angrily]
Why is it?

JANE
It's my birthday.

HANNAH
I didn't know that.

JANE
No, it isn't exactly a national holiday, but we'll have the turkey, and I'll get some preserves up, and I want you to bake a cake, a round one. We'll have candles on it. I got some at the store this morning.

HANNAH [Shocked]
Candles?

JANE
Yes.

HANNAH
Who's going to be to this party?

JANE [A little self-conscious]
Why—just—just ourselves.

HANNAH
Just you and Mr. Ben and Miss Ella?

JANE
Yes.

HANNAH
You don't want candles on that cake, you want crape on it.

[She exits door left.

[JANE crosses up and starts to clear the dining-room table of its red table cover, as **BEN** enters door left.

BEN [Cheerfully]
Well, I fixed Old Nellie up.
[He puts his bottle back in its place in the wall cabinet]
Just got her in time. Thought she was gone for a minute, but she's going to be all right.

JANE
That's good.

[She folds the tablecloth up and puts it away.

BEN [In front of fire]
She knew what I was doin' for her too; you could tell by the way she looked at me! She'll be all right, poor old critter. I remember her when she was a colt, year before I went to high school.

[**JANE** crosses into room, shutting the dining-room door after her.

JANE
You like animals, don't you, Ben?

BEN [Surprised]
I don't know. I don't like to see 'em suffer.

JANE
Why?

BEN
I guess it's mostly because they ain't to blame for it. I mean what comes to 'em ain't their fault. If a woman thinks she's sick, 'til she gets sick, that's her business. If a man gets drunk, or eats like a hog, he's got to pay for it, and he ought to. Animals live cleaner than we do anyhow—and when you do anything for 'em they've got gratitude. Folks haven't.

JANE
Hand me that sewing basket, Ben.

[She has seated herself at left center by table. **BEN** at left of table, hands her the basket as she picks up some sewing.

BEN
It's funny, but except for a dog or two, I don't remember carin' nothin' for any of the live things, when I lived here I mean.

JANE
I guess that's because you didn't do much for them.

BEN
I guess so—Sometimes I kind of think I'd like to be here when spring comes—and see all the young critters coming into the world—I should think there'd be a lot a feller could do, to make it easier for 'em.

JANE
Yes.

BEN
Everybody's always makin' a fuss over women and their babies. I guess animals have got some feelings, too.

JANE [Sewing]

Yes.

BEN
I know it—Yes, sometimes I sort of wish I could be here, in the spring.

JANE
You'll be a big help.

BEN
I'll be in prison.
[He looks at her. She drops her head and goes on sewing]
You forgot that, didn't yer?

JANE
Yes.

BEN
What's the difference? A prison ain't just a place; it's bein' somewheres you don't want to be, and that's where I've always been.

JANE
You liked the army?

BEN
I s'pose so.

JANE
Why?

BEN
I don't know, there was things to do, and you did 'em.

JANE
And some one to tell you what to do?

BEN
Maybe that's it, somebody that knew better'n I did. It galled me at first, but pretty soon we got over in France, an' I saw we was really doin' something, then I didn't mind. I just got to doin' what I was told, and it worked out all right.

JANE
You liked France, too?

BEN
Yes.

JANE
I'd like to hear you tell about it.

BEN
Maybe I'll go back there some time. I don't know as I'd mind farming a place over there. Most of their farms are awful little, but I don't know but what I'd like it.

JANE
Farming is farming. Why not try it here?

BEN
Look out there!
[He points out of the window at the drifted snow]
It's like that half the year, froze up, everything, most of all the people. Just a family by itself, maybe. Just a few folks, good an' bad, month after month, with nothin' to think about but just the mean little things, that really don't amount to nothin', but get to be bigger than all the world outside.

JANE [Sewing]
Somebody must do the farming, Ben.

BEN
Somebody like the Jordans, that's been doin' it generation after generation. Well, look at us. I heard a feller, in a Y.M.C.A. hut, tellin' how nature brought animals into the world, able to face what they had to face—

JANE
Yes, Ben?

BEN
That's what nature's done for us Jordans,—brought us into the world half froze before we was born. Brought us into the world mean, and hard, so's we could live the hard, mean life we have to live.

JANE
I don't know, Ben, but what you could live it different.

BEN
They laugh over there, and sing, and God knows when I was there they didn't have much to sing about. I was at a rest camp, near Nancy, after I got wounded. I told you about the French lady with all those children that I got billeted with.

JANE
Yes.

BEN
They used to sing, right at the table, and laugh! God! It brought a lump into my throat mor'n once, lookin' at them, and rememberin' the Jordans!

JANE
I guess there wasn't much laughing at your family table.

BEN
Summers nobody had much time for it, and winters,—well, I guess you know.

JANE
Yes.

BEN
Just a few folks together, day after day, and every little thing you don't like about the other raspin' on your nerves 'til it almost drives you crazy! Most folks quiet, because they've said all the things they've got to say a hundred times; other folks talkin', talkin', talkin' about nothing. Sometimes somebody sort of laughs, and it scares you; seems like laughter needs the sun, same as flowers do. Icebound, that's what we are all of us, inside and out.

[He stands looking grimly out window.

JANE
Not all. I laughed a lot before I came here to live.

BEN [Turns and looks at her]
I remember, you were just a little girl.

JANE
I was fourteen. See if there's a spool of black sewing cotton in that drawer.

BEN [Looking in drawer]
You mean thread?

JANE
Yes.

BEN
This it?

[He holds up a spool of white thread.

JANE
Would you call that black?

BEN [Looks it over]
No—it ain't black.
[He searches and finds black thread]
Maybe this is it!

JANE
Maybe it is!
[She takes it]
You were with that French family quite a while, weren't you?

BEN
Most a month; they was well off, you know; I mean, they was, before the war. It was a nice house.

JANE [Sewing]
How nice?

BEN [Hesitates]
I don't know, things—well—useful, you know, but nice, not like this.

[He looks about.

JANE [Looks around with a sigh]
It's not very pretty, but it could be. I could make it.

BEN
If you did, folks would be sayin' you wasn't respectable.

JANE
Tell me about the dinner they gave you the night before you went back to your company.

BEN
I told you.

JANE
Tell me again.

BEN [Smiles to himself at the remembrance]
They was all dressed up, the whole family, and there I was with just my dirty old uniform.

JANE
Yes.

BEN [Lost in his recollections]
It was a fine dinner, but it wasn't that. It was their doin' so much for me, folks like that—I've sort of pictured 'em lots of times since then.

JANE
Go on.

BEN
All of the young ones laughing and happy, and the mother too, laughing and tryin' to talk to me, and neither one of us knowing much about what the other one was sayin'.

[He and **JANE** both laugh.

JANE
And the oldest daughter? The one that was most grown up?

BEN
She was scared of me somehow, but I don't know as ever I've seen a girl like her, before or since.

JANE
Maybe 'twas that dress you told me about; seems to me you don't remember much else about her; not so much as what color her hair was, only just that that dress was blue.

BEN [Thoughtfully]
Yes.

JANE [Sewing]
Sometimes you say dark blue!

[She is watching him closely through half-shut eyes.

BEN [Absently]
I guess so.

JANE
And then I say, dark as something I point out to you, that isn't dark at all, and you say, "No, lighter than that!"

BEN [Absently]
Just—sort of blue.

JANE
Yes, sort of blue. It had lace on it, too, didn't it?

BEN
Lace? Maybe—yes, lace.

JANE
There's more than one blue dress in the world.

BEN
Like enough. Maybe there's mor'n one family like that lady's, but I'll be damned if they live in Veazie.
[He crosses and opens cupboard and selects a bottle]
I might as well run out and see how the old mare is getting on.

[He selects bottle from shelf.

JANE
And you've got to shovel those paths for the clothes lines yet.

BEN
I know.

JANE

Well, don't forget.

BEN
It ain't likely you'll let me.

[He exits at door right. **JANE** laughs softly to herself, and runs to closet and takes out a large cardboard box and putting it on the table, she cuts the string and removes the wrapping paper, then lifts the cover of the box and draws out a dainty light-blue gown with soft lace on the neck and sleeves. She holds it up joyfully, then covering her own dress with it, she looks at herself in a mirror on wall. As she stands smiling at her reflection, there is a sharp knock on the outside door. **JANE** hastily returns dress to box and as the knock is repeated, she puts the box under the sofa at left and crosses and opens the outside door.

[**JUDGE BRADFORD** enters.

JANE
Oh, it's you, Judge! Come in.

JUDGE
I thought I'd stop on my way home and see how you were getting on, Jane.

JANE
I'll take your coat.

JUDGE
I'll just put it here.
[He puts coat on chair]
Have you time to sit down a minute?

JANE
Of course.

[They sit.

JUDGE [Looks at her]
That isn't a smile on your lips, is it, Jane?

JANE
Maybe—

JUDGE [Laughingly]
I'm glad I came!

JANE
It's my birthday.

JUDGE
Why, Jane!

[He crosses to her and holds out his hand. She takes it.

Many happy returns!

JANE [Thoughtfully]
Many—happy returns—that's a lot to ask for.

JUDGE
You're about twenty-two, or twenty-three, aren't you?

JANE
Twenty-three.

JUDGE
Time enough ahead of you.

[His eye falls on the box, imperfectly hidden under the sofa; out of it a bit of the blue dress is sticking.

Hello! What's all that?

JANE
My birthday present.

JUDGE
Who gave it to you?

JANE
I did.

JUDGE
Good! It's about time you started to blossom out.

JANE
I ordered a lot of things from Boston; they'll be here to-morrow.

JUDGE
I suppose that one's a dress?

JANE
Yes.

JUDGE [Bends over to look]
Light blue, isn't it?

JANE [Smiles]
Just sort of blue—with lace on it.

JUDGE
Oh, you're going to wear it, I suppose, in honor of your birthday?

JANE [Startled]
To-night—oh, no—soon maybe, but not to-night.

JUDGE [Smiles]
How soon?

JANE
Soon as I dare to; not just yet.

JUDGE
You have plenty of money; you ought to have every comfort in the world, and some of the luxuries.

JANE [Gravely]
Judge! I want you to do something for me.

JUDGE
And of course I'll do it.

JANE
I want you to get Ben off. I want you to fix it so he won't go to State's Prison.

JUDGE
But if he's guilty, Jane?

JANE
I want you to go to old Mr. Kimbal for me and offer to pay him for that barn of his that Ben burned down. Then I want you to fix it so he won't push the case, so's Ben gets off.

JUDGE
Do you know what you are asking of me?

JANE
To get Ben off.

JUDGE
To compound a felony.

JANE
Those are just words, Judge, and words don't matter much to me. I might say I wasn't asking you to compound a felony. I was askin' you to save a sinner, but those would be just words too. There's nobody else; you've got to help me.

JUDGE [Thoughtfully]
I've always thought a lot could be done for Ben, by a good lawyer.

JANE
It doesn't matter how, so long as it's done.

JUDGE
He was drinking, with a crowd of young men; the two Kimbal boys jumped on him and beat him up rather badly. That's about all we know, aside from the fact that Ben was drunk, and that that night the Kimbals' barn was set on fire.

JANE
Just so long as you can get him off, Judge.

JUDGE
I think a case of assault could be made against the Kimbal boys, and I think it would stand.

JANE
What of it?

JUDGE
It is quite possible that the old man, if he knew that action was to be taken against his sons, and if he could be tactfully assured of payment for his barn, say by Ben, in a year's time, might be persuaded to petition to have the indictment against Ben withdrawn. In that event, I think the chances would be very much in Ben's favor.

JANE
I don't care what names you call it, so long as it's done. Will you fix it?

JUDGE
Well, it's not exactly a proper proceeding for a Judge of the Circuit Court.

JANE
I knew you'd do it.

JUDGE
Yes, and I think you knew why, didn't you?

JANE
Ever since she's died, you've helped me about everything. Before she died you were just as good to me, and nobody else was.

JUDGE
I am glad you said that, because it clears me from the charge of being what poor Ben calls "one of the crow buzzards," and I don't want you to think me that.

JANE
No, you're not that.

JUDGE
I love you, Jane.

JANE
No!

JUDGE
Yes—I've done that for a long while. Don't you think you could get used to the thought of being my wife?

JANE [Gently]
No.

JUDGE
I think I could make you happy.

JANE
No.

JUDGE
I am afraid being happy is something you don't know very much about.

JANE
No.

JUDGE
It isn't a thing that I am going to hurry you over, my dear, but neither is it a thing that I am going to give up hoping for.

JANE
When you told me, that day, that Mrs. Jordan had left me all her money, I couldn't understand; then, afterwards, you gave me the letter she left for me. I want you to read it.

JUDGE
What has her letter to do with us?

JANE
Maybe, reading it, you'll get to know something you've got a right to know, better than I could tell it to you.

JUDGE
Very well.

JANE
It's here.

[She opens drawer, and selects a letter in a woman's old-fashioned handwriting, from a large envelope of papers.

She was a cold woman, Judge. She never let me get close to her, although I tried. She didn't love me. I was as sure of it then as I am now.
[She holds out the letter]
Read it.

JUDGE
If it's about the thing I've been speaking of, I'd rather hear it in your voice.

JANE [Reads]
"My dear Jane, the doctor tells me I haven't long to live, and so I'm doing this, the meanest thing I think I've ever done to you. I'm leaving you the Jordan money. Since my husband died, there has been just one person I could get to care about; that's Ben, who was my baby so long after all the others had forgotten how to love me. And Ben's a bad son, and a bad man. I can't leave him the money; he'd squander it, and the Jordans' money came hard."

JUDGE
Poor woman! It was a bitter thing for her to have to write like that.

JANE [Reads on]
"If squandering the money would bring him happiness, I'd face all the Jordans in the other world and laugh at them, but I know there's only just one chance to save my boy,—through a woman who will hold out her heart to him and let him trample on it, as he has on mine."

JUDGE [In sudden fear]
Jane!

JANE [Reads on]
"Who'd work, and pray, and live for him, until as age comes on, and maybe he gets a little tired, he'll turn to her. And you're that woman, Jane; you've loved him ever since you came to us. Although he doesn't even know it. The Jordan name is his, the money's yours, and maybe there'll be another life for you to guard. God knows it isn't much I'm leaving you, but you can't refuse it, because you love him, and when he knows the money is yours, he will want to marry you. I'm a wicked old woman. Maybe you'll learn to forgive me as time goes on—It takes a long time to make a Jordan."
[**JANE** drops her hand to her side]
Then she just signed her name.

JUDGE
Is the damnable thing she says there true?

JANE
Yes, Judge.

JUDGE
And you're going to do this thing for her?

JANE
No, for him.

JUDGE [Bitterly]
He isn't worth it.

JANE
I guess you don't understand.

JUDGE
No.

[He crosses and picks up his coat.

JANE
You can't go like that, angry. You have to pay a price for being a good man, Judge—I need your help.

JUDGE
You mean he needs my help?

JANE
Yes, and you'll have to give it to him, if what you said a little while ago was true.

JUDGE [After a pause]
It was true, Jane. I'll help him.

[He picks up his hat.

JANE
I've an errand at the store. I'll go with you.

[She takes hat and coat from rack and puts them on.

JUDGE
Is it anything I could have sent up for you?

JANE [Putting on coat]
I guess not. You see, I've got to match a color.

JUDGE
Another new dress?

JANE [They start toward door]
Just a ribbon, for my hair.

JUDGE
I didn't know women still wore ribbons in their hair.

JANE
It seems they do—in France.

[They exit together at left to the outside door and off.

[**NETTIE** and **ELLA** enter quickly, after a slight pause, Nettie running in from right, followed more sedately by **ELLA**.

NETTIE
You see! I was right! She went with him.

[She has run to window left and is looking out.

ELLA
That's what money does. If mother hadn't left her everything, he wouldn't have touched her with a ten-foot pole.

NETTIE
Well, if she's fool enough to stay in this place, I guess he's about the best there is.

ELLA
Then trust her for gettin' him; by the time she gets through in Veazie, this town will be barer than Mother Hubbard's cupboard by the time the dog got there.
[Her eye falls on Jane's box, partly under sofa.]
What's that?

[She bends over, looking at it.

NETTIE
What?

ELLA
I never saw it before.
[She draws it out]
Looks like a dress. See! Blue silk!

NETTIE
Open it.

ELLA [Hesitates]
Must be hers! Maybe she wouldn't like it.

NETTIE
Maybe she wouldn't know it.

ELLA
A cat can look at a king!

[She opens the box and holds up the blue dress.

NETTIE

Oh! Oh!

ELLA [Really moved]
Some folks would say a dress like that wasn't decent, but I wouldn't care, not if it was mine, and it might have been mine—but for her.

NETTIE
Yours! Grandma wouldn't have left her money to you. She hated old people. Everybody does. She'd have left it to me, but for Jane Crosby!

ELLA [Looks at dress]
I always wanted a dress like this; when I was young, I used to dream about one, but mother only laughed. For years I counted on gettin' me what I wanted, when she died; now I never will.

NETTIE [Fiercely]
I will—somehow!

ELLA
Maybe but not me. Oh, if I could have the feelin' of a dress like that on me, if I could wear it once, where folks could see me—Just once! Oh, I know how they'd laugh—I wouldn't care—

NETTIE [Almost in tears]
I can't stand it if she's going to wear things like that.

ELLA
I'll put it back.

[She starts to do so.

NETTIE [Catches her hand]
Not yet.

ELLA
I guess the less we look at it, the better off we'll be.

[There is a ring at the front door.

NETTIE
Who's that?

ELLA
Here!
[She hands the box to **NETTIE**]
Shove it back under the sofa. I'll go and see.

[She turns and crosses to door left and out to the vestibule. **NETTIE**, with the box in her arms, hesitates for a moment then turns and exits at right, taking the box with her. **ELLA** opens the outside door at left, showing **ORIN** on the doorstep. **ELLA** looks at him angrily.

For time's sake, what are you ringing the bell for?

ORIN
Mum says for me not to act like I belonged here.

ELLA
Well, I'm goin' to shut the door. Git in or git out!

ORIN
I got a note.
[He enters room as **ELLA** shuts door]
It's for her.

ELLA [Holds out hand]
Let me see it.

ORIN
Mum said not to let on I had nothin' if you came nosin' around.

[**JANE** enters from left.

JANE
I just ran across to the store. I haven't been five minutes.

[She takes coat off.

ELLA
He's got a note for you, from Sadie.

JANE
Oh, let me see it, Orin.

ORIN [Gives her note]
She said, if you said is they an answer, I was to say yes, they is.

JANE
Just a minute.

[She opens note and reads it.

ELLA
I must say she didn't lose much time.

JANE [After reading note]
Poor Sadie! Wait, Orin!

[She sits at table and takes checkbook from the drawer and writes.

Just take this to your mother.

ELLA
You don't mean you're goin' to—

JANE
Be quiet, Ella. Here, Orin.
[She hands him check]
Don't lose it, and run along.

ORIN
All right. Mum said we was goin' to have dinner early, and go to a movie! Good night.

JANE [Again writing in checkbook]
Good night.

[**ORIN** exits.

ELLA
So you sent her her rent money, after all?

JANE
Here!

[She rises and hands a check to **ELLA**.

ELLA
What's that?

JANE
Two hundred dollars. You can try that dressmaking business if you want to, Ella.

ELLA [Looks at check]
Two hundred dollars!

JANE
You needn't thank me.

ELLA
That ain't it. I was just wonderin' what's come over you all of a sudden.

[**BEN** enters.

JANE
It's my birthday, that's all. Did you know it was my birthday, Ben?

BEN [Carelessly]

Is it? I shoveled them damned paths!

[He crosses and sits by fire.

JANE
Ella's going into the dressmaking business, Ben.

BEN [Moodily]
What of it?

ELLA
That's what I say. It ain't much of a business.

[She exits at right; outside it grows to dusk.

JANE
Are you tired?

BEN
Maybe.

[He stretches his feet out toward fire.

JANE
You've done a lot of work to-day.

BEN
And every day.

JANE
I don't suppose you know how much good it's done you, how well you look!

BEN
Beauty's only skin deep.

JANE
Folks change, even in a few weeks, outside and in. Hard work don't hurt anybody.

BEN
I got chilblains on my feet. The damned shoes are stiffer than they ever was.

JANE
Icebound, you said. Maybe it don't have to be like that. Sometimes, just lately, it's seemed to me that if folks would try, things needn't be so bad. All of 'em try, I mean, for themselves, and for everybody else.

BEN
If I was you, I'd go out somewheres and hire a hall.

JANE
If you'd put some pork fat on those shoes to-night, your feet wouldn't hurt so bad.

BEN
Maybe.

[He sits looking moodily into the fire. After a moment's hesitation, Jane crosses and sits in the chair beside his, the evening shadows deepen around them but the glow from the fire lights their faces.

JANE
I'm lonesome to-night. We always made a lot of birthdays when I was a girl.

BEN
Some do.

JANE
Your mother didn't. She found me once trying, the day I was fifteen. I remember how she laughed at me.

BEN
All the Jordans have got a sense of humor.

JANE
She wasn't a Jordan, not until she married your father.

BEN
When a woman marries into a family, she mostly shuts her eyes and jumps in all over.

JANE
Your mother was the best of the whole lot of you. Anyway, I think so.

BEN
I know it. I always thought a lot of her, in spite of our being relations.

JANE
She loved you, Ben.

BEN
She left me without a dollar, knowin' I was going to State's Prison, and what I'd be by the time I get out.

JANE
Maybe some day you'll understand why she did it.

BEN
Because she thought you'd take better care of the money than any of the rest of us.

JANE
And you hate me because of that, the way all the rest of the Jordans do?

BEN
Sometimes.

JANE [Sadly]
I suppose it's natural.

BEN
But I ain't such a fool as Henry, and the women folks. They think you took advantage and fooled her into what she did. I thought so at first, now I don't.

JANE
What do you think now, Ben?

BEN
She'd watched you; she knew you were worth mor'n all of us in a lump. I know it, too, but some way it riles me worse than if you wasn't.

JANE
That's silly!

BEN [With growing resentment]
Don't you suppose I know what you've been doin' to me. Tryin' to make a man of me. Tryin' to help me. Standing up to me and fightin' me every day, tryin' to teach me to be decent. Workin' over me like I was a baby, or somethin', and you was tryin' to teach me how to walk. Gettin' me so upset that every time I don't do what I ought to do, I get all het up inside; I never was so damned uncomfortable in all my life.

JANE
And I never was so happy.

BEN
I s'pose God knew what he was about when he made women.

JANE
Of course he did.

BEN
Anyhow, he gave 'em the best of it, all right.

JANE
You don't mean that! You can't!

BEN
I do. Let a man get miserable, and he is miserable. A woman ain't really happy no other way.

JANE
Maybe you think I'm having an easier time right now than you are.

BEN
I know it.

JANE
They all hate me, and they all want something, all the time. I can't say yes, and it's hard to always say no. Then there's the farm, big, and poor, and all worked out. The Jordans have been taking their living out of this soil for more than a hundred years, and never putting anything back.

BEN
Just themselves, that's all.

JANE
Worked right, like they do out West, this place could be what it ought to be. How can I do that; it needs a man.

BEN
I been thinkin' lately things could be done a whole lot different.

JANE
By a man, if he loved the old place— You Jordans robbed this soil always. Suppose one of you tried to pay it back—it would mean work and money, for a couple of years maybe, then I guess you'd see what gratitude meant.

BEN
It could be done; it ought to be.

JANE
By you, Ben!

BEN
No—I guess I ain't got the judgment.

JANE
You've got it, if you'd learn to use it.

BEN
Anyhow, I've got just a month, that's all.

JANE
Maybe you'll have more.

BEN
I'm as good as convicted as I sit here. I've only got a month.

JANE
Then help me for that month. We could plan how to start out in the spring. I've got books that will help us, and I can get more. We could do a lot!

BEN
I don't know but what we could!

JANE [Bends toward him]
Will you shake hands on it?

[She offers her hand.

BEN [Surprised]
What for?

JANE
Oh, just because we never have.

BEN
We ain't goin' to change everything, are we?

JANE
One thing. We're going to be friends.

BEN [Takes her hand awkwardly]
You're a good sport, game as a man, gamer maybe.

JANE
And now for the surprise.

BEN
The what!

JANE [Draws her hand away and rises]
You'll see. I want you to sit right here, until I open those doors.

[She points to doors to dining room.

BEN
I wasn't thinkin' of movin'.

JANE
Just sit right there.

BEN
And do what?

JANE
Think.

BEN
What of?

JANE
Oh, anything—so long as it's pleasant—of the spring that's coming—

BEN
In the prison down at Thomaston.

JANE
Of France then, of the family that was so good to you—of the beautiful lady—of the daughter, if you want to, the one that was most grown up—and of the wonderful blue dress. Just shut your eyes and think, 'til I come back!

[She exits through doors to dining room and closes the doors after her. **BEN** sits in glow from the fire, his eyes closed. In a moment the door at right is thrown open and **NETTIE** stands in the doorway, the light from the hall falling on her. She has on Jane's blue dress and is radiant with youth and excitement.

NETTIE
Ben! Look at me! Look, Ben!

BEN
What?

NETTIE
Look Ben!

[He looks at her and for a moment sits in stupid wonder, then rises slowly to his feet.

BEN
It's—It's Nettie!

NETTIE
Did you ever see anything so lovely, did you?

BEN
You're—you're a woman, Nettie!

NETTIE
Of course I am, you stupid!

BEN [Crosses down to her]
God! How I've starved for somethin' pretty to look at! God! How I've starved for it!

NETTIE
That's why I came down, I wanted you to see! I waited there in the hall till she went out.

BEN
And you've been here all the time, and I haven't so much as looked at you!

NETTIE [Softly]
You've been in trouble, Ben!

BEN
I'll get out of that somehow! I'm going to make a fight. I ain't goin' to let 'em take me now.

NETTIE
Honest, Ben?

BEN
Not now. Oh, you pretty kid! You pretty little thing!

[He catches her fiercely in his arms.

NETTIE
You mustn't, Ben!

BEN [Triumphant]
Mustn't! You don't know me!

NETTIE
Just one then!

[She holds up her lips, and as he kisses her ardently, the dining-room doors back of them open and **JANE** stands in the doorway, looking at them. She has removed her apron and has made some poor attempt at dressing up. Back of her we see the table bravely spread for the festive birthday party. There is a large turkey and other special dishes, and a round cake on which blaze twenty-two tiny candles. They turn their heads, startled, as **JANE** looks at them, and **BEN** tightens his arms defiantly about **NETTIE**.

Let me go!

BEN [Holding her and looking past her to **JANE**]
No!
[Then to **JANE**]
Why are you looking at me like that?

NETTIE
Let me go.

BEN [To **JANE**]
To hell with your dream of grubbing in the dirt. Now I know what I want, and I'm going to get it.

NETTIE
Let go, dear.
[She draws away]
I'm ashamed about wearin' your dress, Cousin Jane. I'll take it right off.

JANE

You needn't. I guess I don't want it any more.

[For the first time her eyes leave **BEN'S** face. She turns and steps past them to the door at right and calls]

Supper's ready, Ella!

[**HANNAH** enters at back in dining room with a plate of hot biscuits.

ACT III

SCENE: Same as Act One. Parlor at the Jordans', two months later.

At rise the characters are grouped exactly as they were at the opening of the play. The white slip covers, however, have been removed from the chairs, and the backing through the window shows partly melted snow drifts. **HENRY** sighs; the clock strikes two. **HENRY** looks at his watch.

There is a pause. The outside door slams and **BEN** enters and looks about.

BEN
Well—here we all are again.

SADIE [Sadly]
Yes.

HENRY
I ain't been in this room before since the funeral.

SADIE
And I ain't, and the last time before that was when father died.

EMMA
I sat right here, in the same chair I'm settin' in now, but to your grandfather's funeral, right after I married Henry, I was treated like one of the poor relations! I had to stand up.

HENRY
I remember; it made considerable trouble.

ELLA
I don't know as it was ever what I called a cheerful room.

HENRY [Severely]
A parlor's where a person's supposed to sit and think of God, and you couldn't expect it to be cheerful!

ELLA [Looks about]

Seems like we'd had trouble and disgrace enough in this family without her takin' all the slip covers off of the chairs and sofa!

EMMA
It ain't right!

SADIE
That Boston woman that's building the house over on Elm Street ain't so much as goin' to have a parlor. I stopped her right on the street and asked her what she was plannin' to do soon as the first of 'em died.

EMMA
What did she say?

SADIE
Said she tried not to think about such things.

HENRY [Sternly]
We got Atheists enough in this town right now.

BEN
Well, if Jane's coming I wish she'd come; this ain't exactly my idea of pleasant company.

ELLA
She says we're all to wait in here for Judge Bradford.

SADIE
What did she send for us for?

ELLA
I don't know.

EMMA
Why didn't you ask her?

ELLA
I did, and she most bit my head off.

BEN
She most bites mine off every time I see her. I must say she's changed, Jane has; she ain't the same girl at all she was a few weeks ago.

NETTIE
She's actin' just awful, especially to me!

SADIE
Of course, I'd be the last one to say anything against her, but—

BEN

But nothin'! There ain't one of you here fit to tie her shoes!

SADIE
We ain't?

BEN
And I ain't! The only difference between us is I ain't worth much and I know it, and you ain't worth nothin' and you don't.

EMMA
I guess you'd better be careful how you talk!

NETTIE
If anybody says anything about Jane lately, that's the way he always talks! The worse she treats him the better he seems to like it.

SADIE
Well, I don't know as I'm surprised more about his insultin' the rest of us, but it's sort of comical his talkin' that way about you, Nettie.

EMMA
Nettie! What's Nettie got to do with him?

SADIE
Oh! Excuse me! I didn't know 'twas supposed to be a secret.

EMMA
What is?

SADIE
About the way those two have been carryin' on together!

HENRY
What!

ELLA
Ben and Nettie!

NETTIE [Afraid]
Stop her, Ben, can't you?

BEN
If I knew a way to stop women like her I'd patent it and get rich!

EMMA [Sternly]
Him and Nettie?

SADIE

They passed my house together once a week ago Wednesday, once the Tuesday before that, and twice the Sunday after New Year's.

HENRY
Together!

SADIE
And Eben Tilden's boy told Abbie Palsey that Tilly Hickson heard Aaron Hamlin say he'd seen 'em together at the picture show!

HENRY [To **BEN**]
Is it true?

EMMA
You've been with him after all I told you!

BEN
It ain't going to hurt her none just to talk to me, is it?

EMMA
Them that touches pitch gets defiled!

HENRY [To **NETTIE**]
I want you to tell me everything that's took place between you two.

SADIE
Wait!

HENRY
What?

SADIE
Orin! Leave the room!

NETTIE
He don't have to leave the room. I don't care who knows what happened!

HENRY
Go on then.

NETTIE
Well—Ben and I—We—Just for a few days—anyway, it was all his fault.

BEN
She threw me down because I was going to prison.

NETTIE
He said he'd get out of it somehow, but he can't, and I just won't have folks laughing at me!

BEN
It's all right, it never meant nothin' to her, and I guess it didn't mean much to me. It's just as well it's over.

NETTIE
It's a whole lot better.

HENRY
Well—what's passed is passed. Folks that plant the wind reap the whirlwind! There's no use cryin' over spilled milk.

ORIN
Say, Mum! What do you s'pose Uncle Henry thinks he means when he says things?

HENRY
Somehow I can't help wishin' you was my son for just about five minutes.

[**HANNAH** and **JUDGE BRADFORD** enter.

HANNAH
They're all in here, Judge.

JUDGE
Good afternoon.

HENRY
How are you, Judge?

SADIE
It's a mild day; winter's most over. Stop scratching yourself.

[This last to **ORIN** who seems to be uneasy and frequently scratches himself.

HANNAH [At door]

I'll tell her you're here, Judge. She'll be right down.

[**HANNAH** exits.

ELLA
Won't you sit?

JUDGE
Thanks.

[He sits by table.

HENRY
What's it about? Why did she say we was to all be here at two o'clock?

JUDGE
She will probably be able to answer that question herself, Ben.

SADIE [To **ORIN**]
Don't.

ORIN
What?

SADIE
Scratch!

ORIN
Oh.

[**JANE** enters. The **JUDGE** rises.

JUDGE
Well, Jane?

JANE
Don't get up, Judge.

JUDGE
Will you sit here?

[**JUDGE** turns to get a chair for **JANE**. **ORIN** scratches himself. **ELLA** rises.

ELLA
What is the matter with this brat?

ORIN
I itch!

SADIE
It's warm, and he's got on his heavy flannels! He's as clean as you are!

[**JANE** and **JUDGE** sit.

BEN
You said to heat this room up and wait here for you and the Judge. Why? I got my stock to tend.

HENRY
It's a bad time for me to get away from the store; What was it you wanted of us?

JANE
I'm afraid it isn't going to be easy to tell you.

JUDGE
Won't you let me do it, Jane?

JANE
No. I've come to know that your mother didn't really want that I should have the Jordan money.

SADIE
What's that?

JANE
I put it as simply as I could.

BEN
You mean a later will's been found?

JUDGE
No.

JANE
In a way, Judge, it's like there had. Your mother left me a letter dated later than the will.

ELLA
Leavin' the money different?

JANE
Tellin' what she really wanted.

BEN
Well, what did she want?

JANE
It was like she left me all her money in trust, so I could keep it safe until the time she was hopin' for come, and in a way it did come, not quite like she wanted it, but near enough so I can give up a burden I haven't strength enough to carry any more.

[She stops.

JUDGE
Let me finish, Jane. Jane has asked me to draw a deed of gift, making the Jordan property over to Ben.

BEN
Why?

JANE
She wanted you to have it.

BEN
Why didn't she will it to me, then?

JANE
She was afraid to trust you.

BEN
Well?

JANE
You've learned to work; you'll keep on working.

HENRY
You mean to say my mother wanted him to have it all?

JANE
Yes.

HENRY
I am a religious man, but there was a time when even Job gave up! So—all our money goes to Ben—and he can't even buy himself out of prison!

JANE [After a pause]
Ben isn't going to prison.

BEN
Why? Who's to stop it?

JUDGE [After a look from **JANE**]
Kimbal agreed not to press the charge against you. It seems that there were certain extenuating circumstances. A motion has been made for the dismissal of the indictment, and it won't be opposed.

BEN
Why did he? Who fixed this thing.

JANE
Judge Bradford did.

[She looks at **JUDGE**.

BEN [Slowly]
It means a lot to me. There's things I'd like to do. I haven't dared to think about 'em lately—now I'll do 'em.

[There is a pause.

HENRY

Well, Ben, so you've got the money! I guess maybe it's better than her havin' it; after all blood's thicker than water! We'll help you any way we can and—er—of course you'll help us.

BEN
Why will I?

HENRY
We're brothers, Ben! We're old Jordans!

BEN
What was we when I got back from France? There was a band met us boys at the station. I was your brother all right that day, only somehow, in just a little while you forgot about it. I was a Jordan when I was hidin' out from the police, and all that kept me from starvin' was the money Jane sent me! I was your brother the night mother died, and you said you wouldn't go my bail.

ELLA
You ain't going to be hard, Ben!

BEN
I'm the head of the family now, ain't I, and you can bet all you've got I'm going to be a real Jordan.

HENRY
I think, Ben—

BEN
From now on, there ain't nobody got any right to think in this house but just me! So run along home, the whole pack of you, and after this, when you feel like you must come here—come separate.

ELLA
Turn us out, Ben?

BEN
Sure, why not?

NETTIE [Crosses to him. Sweetly]
There ain't any reason why we can't be friends, is there?

BEN
Well, I don't know. There's only one way I could ever get to trust you.

NETTIE
What way, Ben?

BEN
I'd have to go to jail for five years and see if you'd wait for me!

EMMA
It's an awful thing for a mother to have a fool for a child.

ELLA [Goes upstage with **NETTIE**]
Well, I must say you made a nice mess of things!

NETTIE [Exits with **ELLA**]
Well, I don't care! I don't see how anybody would expect me to be a mind reader!

SADIE
Come, Orin—say good-by to your Uncle Ben.

ORIN
What will I do that for?

SADIE
Because I tell you to!

ORIN
Yesterday you told me he wasn't worth speakin' to!

SADIE
Are you going to move, you stupid little idiot.

[She drags him out.

ORIN [As they go]
What did I say? You let me alone!

HENRY
I was wonderin', Ben, how you'd feel about endorsing that note of mine.

BEN
You was?

HENRY
Yes, I don't know what I'm going to do about it.

BEN
As far as I care, you can go nail it on a door.

[**HENRY** and **EMMA** start to exit.

No, hold on, I'll pay it.

HENRY
You will!

BEN
Yes, I don't know as it would do me much good at the bank, havin' a brother of mine in the poorhouse.

[**BEN** laughs as **HENRY** and **EMMA** exit.

JUDGE
Well, Ben? "Uneasy lies the head that wears a crown."

BEN [Down to stove]
Depends on the head. Mine's thick, I guess. Anyhow, none of them is going to bother it. I'm boss here now.

JUDGE
You'll find a copy here of the inventory of the estate, and other legal papers. Everything is in order.

JANE
And my accounts, Ben; you'll find the exact amount your mother left. I spent some money about six weeks ago, on myself, but I've been careful ever since and I've made up for it.

BEN
You said, Judge, she didn't have to go by that letter of my mother's, if she didn't want to? She didn't have to give anything back at all?

JUDGE
No, she didn't.

BEN
Then if I was you—
[To **JANE**]
I wouldn't talk so much about the little you spent on yourself. I guess to look at you it wasn't much.

JANE
Yes, it was.

BEN
Well, we'll fix things so you can keep on spendin'. Only let's see somethin' come of it. I never was so damned sick of anything in my life as I am of that old black dress of yours!

[Crosses stage up and over right.

JANE
I've got plenty of clothes upstairs. I'm sorry now I ever bought them, but I'll take them with me when I go.

BEN
Go? Go where?

JANE
To Old Town. I've got a place there, clerking in the Pulp Mill.

BEN
You!

JANE
Yes.

BEN
But what about me?

JUDGE
Don't you think Jane has done about enough for you?

BEN
She's done a lot, she's given up the money. I don't know as I like that; 'course I like gettin' it, but not if she's going away.

JANE
I couldn't stay now, and I wouldn't want to.

BEN
I don't suppose you remember about plannin' what you and me was to do with this old farm?

JANE
I remember.

BEN
Well—then what are you going away for?

JANE
Because I couldn't be happy here, Ben—It's been harder than anything I ever thought could come to anybody, the last few weeks here—and so I'm going. [She turns to Judge] I'll go upstairs and get my things. I'll stop at your office, Judge, on the way to the station.

JUDGE
Thank you, Jane.

BEN
You're goin' to-day? Before I order my new farm machinery or anything? You're goin' to leave me with all this work on my hands?

JANE
Yes, Ben.

[She exits.

BEN
Well—that's a lesson to me! Oh, she's a good woman! I ain't denyin' that—but she's fickle!

JUDGE
You're a fool, Ben!

BEN
I been doin' kitchen police around this town for quite a spell now, Judge, but from this day on I ain't goin' to take that sort of talk from anybody.

JUDGE
I assure you that you won't have to take any sort of talk at all from me.

[He starts for the door.

BEN
I didn't mean that. I don't want you to think I ain't grateful for all you've done for me.

JUDGE [Coldly]
I have done nothing for you.

BEN
If it wasn't for you, I'd want to die; that's what I did want. I was afraid of that prison, just a coward about it. Now I'm a free man, with a big life openin' out ahead of me—I got everything in the world right here in my two hands, everything—and I owe it to you!

JUDGE
I am very glad to say that you don't owe me anything. I don't like you, I haven't forgiven you for what you did to your mother's life. Nor for a worse thing, one you haven't brains enough to even know you've done. Don't be grateful to me, Ben, please. I think nothing could distress me more than that.

BEN
You've been a good friend to me.

JUDGE
I haven't meant to be, as I said I don't like you. I haven't any faith in you. I don't believe in this new life of yours. You made a mess of the old one, and I think you will of the new.

BEN
No matter what you say, you can't get away from me. I'll be grateful till I die. But for you I'd have gone to that damned prison!

JUDGE
But for Jane.

BEN
How Jane?

JUDGE
How Jane? Jane went your bond the day your mother died. Jane took you in and taught you how to work, made you work, taught you through the one decent spot in you something of a thing you'd never

know, self-respect. Worked over you, petted you, coaxed you—held you up—Then you hurt her—but she kept on—She went herself to Kimbal, after he had refused me, and got his help to keep you out of prison—then, against my will, against the best that I could do to stop her, she turns over all this to you—and goes out with nothing—and you ask "How Jane?"

BEN
Why? Why has she done this, all this, for me?

[The **JUDGE** looks at **BEN** with contempt and turns and exits. **BEN** is left in deep thought. **JANE** comes downstairs dressed for a journey with a hand bag, etc. She enters.

JANE
Good-by, Ben.
[She crosses to him, her hand out]
Good-by. Won't you say good-by?

BEN
First, there's some things I got to know about.

JANE [Smiles]
I guess there's not much left for us to say, Ben.

BEN [She crosses to door, but he gets ahead of her]
There's things I got to know.
[She looks at him but does not speak]
The Judge tells me 'twas you got Kimbal to let me go free.
[He looks at her—she half turns away]
Answer me.
[Pause]
The Judge tells me you gave up what was yours—to me—without no other reason than because you wanted me to have it. That's true, ain't it?
[Pause]
You sent me every cent you had, when you knew mother was dying, then you went bail for me, like he said—and did all them other things. I don't know as any woman ever did any more—. I want to know why!

JANE
Why do you think?

BEN
I don't know—I sort of thought—sort of hoped—

JANE [Bravely]
It was because I loved her, Ben—

BEN
Oh.

[He turns away disappointed.

JANE
You're forgetting, I guess, how long we was alone here—when you was in France—then the months we didn't know where you was, when the police was looking for you—She used to make me promise if ever I could I'd help you.

BEN
Well—all I've got to say is you're no liar.

JANE
Good-by.

[She turns to go.

BEN
Wait.
[Closes door]
Let's see that letter you said she left for you.

JANE
No. I won't do that. I've done enough; you're free, you've got the money and the farm.

BEN [Crosses in front of table and sits left of table]
They ain't worth a damn with you gone—I didn't know that till just now, but they ain't.

JANE
It's sort of sudden, the way you found that out.

BEN
Oh, it don't take long for a man to get hungry—it only takes just a minute for a man to die; you can burn down a barn quick enough, or do a murder; it's just living and getting old that takes a lot of time—Can't you stay here, Jane?

JANE
There's Nettie.

BEN
Nettie—that couldn't stand the gaff—that run out on me when I was in trouble.

JANE
It doesn't matter what folks do, if you love 'em enough.

BEN
What do you know about it? I suppose you've been in love a lot of times?

JANE
No.

BEN

Then you be quiet and let an expert talk. I was lonesome and I wanted a woman; she was pretty and I wanted to kiss her—that ain't what I call love.

JANE

You. You don't even know the meaning of the word.

BEN

That don't worry me none—I guess the feller that wrote the dictionary was a whole lot older'n I am before he got down to the L's.

JANE

You've got good in you, Ben, deep down, if you'd only try.
[**BEN** turns]
I know, it's always been that way! You've never tried for long; you've never had a real ambition.

BEN

When I was a kid I wanted to spit farther than anybody.

JANE

Good-by.

[She starts up to door.

BEN

And so you're going to break your word?

[**JANE**, hurt—turns]

BEN

I don't know what 'twas you promised mother, but you've broke your word. No man ever needed a woman more'n I need you, and you're leaving me.

JANE

That isn't fair.

BEN

It's true, ain't it; truth ain't always fair—You ain't helped me none, you've hurt me—worse than being broke, worse than bein' in jail.

JANE

It don't seem like I could stand to have you talk like that.

BEN

What you done you done for her. I didn't count, I never have, not with you.

JANE

When you've been trying to do a thing as long as I have, it gets to be a part of you.

BEN
You done it all for her—well—she's dead—you'd better go.

JANE
Maybe I had, but if I do it will be with the truth between us. Here's the letter she left for me, Ben—I got a feeling somehow like she was here with us now, like she wanted you to read it.
[She holds it out]
It's like she was guiding us from the grave—Read it.

[Crosses up to window.

BEN [Reads]
"My dear Jane: The doctor tells me I haven't long to live and so I am doing this, the meanest thing I think I've ever done to you. I'm leaving you the Jordan money. Since my husband died there has been just one person I could get to care about, that's Ben, who was my baby so long after all the others had forgotten how to love me."
[He mumbles the letter to himself, then brings out the words]
"Hold out her heart and let him trample on it, as he has on mine."

[Slowly he breaks down, sobbing bitterly.

JANE
Don't, Ben—

BEN
Look what I done to her. Look what I done.

JANE [Hand on his shoulder]
Oh, my dear—my dear!

BEN
I did love her, mor'n she thought, mor'n I ever knew how to tell her!

JANE [Kneels beside him]
It wasn't all your fault—you were a lonely boy—she never said much—she was like you, Ben, ashamed to show the best that's in you.

BEN [Bitterly]
The best in me. I ain't fit that you should touch me Jane—you'd better go.

JANE
Not if you need me, Ben, and I think you do.

BEN
I love you—mor'n I ever thought I could—tenderer—truer—but I'm no good—You couldn't trust me—I couldn't trust myself.

JANE
Spring's coming, Ben, everywhere, to you and me, if you would only try.

BEN
Can a feller change—Just 'cause he wants to?

JANE
I don't want you changed. I want you what you are, the best of you—just a man that loves me—if you do love me, Ben.

BEN
Can't you help me to be fit?

JANE
I'm going to do the thing I always meant to do—Good times and bad, Ben, I'm going to share with you.

BEN
God knows I—

JANE
Hush, Ben—I don't want another promise.

BEN
What do you want?

JANE
You said I was a good sport once—You shook hands on what we'd do to bring this old place back—there's plenty to be done. I'll stay and help you if you want me.

BEN
A good sport?
[He takes her hand]
I'll say you're all of that.

[**HANNAH** enters.

HANNAH
If you ain't careful you'll miss that train.

JANE
That's just what I want to do.

HANNAH
You ain't going?

JANE
I'm never going, Hannah.

HANNAH
You going to marry him?

BEN
You bet your life she is!

HANNAH
I guess you'll be mighty happy—marriage changes folks—and any change in him will be a big improvement.

[She picks up Jane's bag and exits—**JANE** and **BEN** laugh.

www.ingramcontent.com/pod-product-compliance
Lightning Source LLC
Chambersburg PA
CBHW060035050426
42448CB00012B/3018